# Introduction

Mission Alive Discipleship Cohorts are small groups of disciples who encourage each other by sharing how God is transforming their lives through Scripture, prayer, and mission. The cohorts meet weekly either online or in-person with a facilitator trained to emphasize listening to one another, keeping the conversation flowing, and protecting a safe, comfortable, open environment for growth. The facilitator is not a leader, teacher, or mentor seeking to pass on information or impose their views. Instead, DC facilitators are co-participants on the journey of discipleship committed to allowing God to work through every individual through the work of the Spirit.

This eBook contains the materials and session assignments for an initial 16-week discipleship cohort. After the initial 16-week journey, cohorts can continue to meet and practice the balanced discipleship rhythms of listening to God through Scripture, prayer, and mission as they share life in an authentic community pursuing the mission of Christ.

Whether you have been a Christian for years or are just considering a new life in Christ, discipleship cohorts are designed to help you develop a deeper relationship with God. To join an online group or locate a group in your area, visit **https://missionalive.org/discipleship-cohorts or email Mission Alive at contact@missionalive.org.**

# About Mission Alive

Mission Alive is a missional church planting and discipleship ministry that focuses on innovative church planting in North America. Since 2004, Mission Alive has been assessing, training, and coaching creative leaders to start innovative churches especially in marginalized communities

After several years of starting new churches, we discovered the need to train leaders to start intentionally reproducing discipleship groups, and Discipleship Cohorts were born. Discipleship Cohorts have reproduced in a variety of locations from Mission Alive church plants to Christian college campuses and campus ministries to Hispanic communities and youth ministries.

Besides starting new, innovative churches and intentionally reproducing discipleship groups, Mission Alive also trains leaders to use a leadership coaching posture to help others grow through a ministry called Catalyze Coaching. Catalyze Coaching trains leaders to come alongside others, help them identify goals, and then work step-by-step toward accomplishing the goal. Along the way, they experience growth in many ways.

To contact Mission Alive go to www.missionalive.org or email us at contact@missionalive.org.

# Mission Alive
# Discipleship Cohorts

(Adult Disciple Version)

A facilitated small-group journey of disciples learning to listen to God through Scripture, Prayer, and Mission

General Editor

Stephen Shaffer

Authors

Steven Carrizal

Jeremy Hoover

Lantz Howard

Stephen Shaffer

Tod K. Vogt

Version

4.2

June 2021

# Notices

Mission Alive

PO Box 794302

Dallas, TX, 75379

www.MissionAlive.org

# Contents

# Orientation

Your journey to establish healthy discipleship rhythms listening to God through scripture, prayer, and mission will start with a 16-week facilitated small group meeting. Before each session, you should complete the assignments listed for that week. In each session, your facilitator will guide a conversation where everyone participates, responding to what God is saying through scripture, prayer, mission, and the weeks assignments. There are no right or wrong answers. There are no expectations for perfection--just a shared desire to be disciples learning to let God take the lead in our life.

## Orientation (complete before your first cohort meeting)

- Read What is a Discipleship Cohort (DC)

- Read Perspectives on Discipleship by S. Shaffer

- Read DC Commitment Pledge

- Use the Spiritual Journey Timeline Template to graph your spiritual journey

## Articles

*What Is a Discipleship Cohort?*

*Perspectives on Discipleship by S. Shaffer*

*DC Commitment Pledge*

*Spiritual Journey Timeline Template to graph your spiritual journey*

# Month 1
# Listening to God Through Scripture

## Week 1
- Read Listening for God's Voice by S. Shaffer

- Read Spirit or Self by T. Vogt

- Journal about your reflections from the articles. What do you hear God saying to you through these readings? What are your aha moments? What are you noticing about your relationship with God?

## Week 2
- Read Listening to God through Scripture by S. Carrizal.

- Practice one form of Listening to God through Scripture 2-3 times this week and journal about your experience.

## Week 3
- Practice one form of Listening to God through Scripture 2-3 times this week following your cohorts' selected reading schedule. Journal about your experience.

## Week 4
- Practice one form of Listening to God through Scripture 2-3 times this week following your cohorts selected reading schedule. Journal about your experience.

- Read Adopting a Mission Space

- Choose a Mission Space and spend at least 1 hour there praying and observing. If you have the opportunity, invite someone in the Mission Space to try one of the Listening to God through Scripture exercises. Journal about your experience.

## Articles

# Month 2
## Listening to God Through Prayer

## Week 1
- Read Identity in Christ by S. Shaffer.

- Complete the New Identity in Christ worksheet.

- Practice one form of Listening to God through Scripture 2-3 times this week and journal about your experience.

## Week 2
- Read Listening to God through Prayer by S. Carrizal.

- Watch the video "Being the Beloved" by Henri Nouwen on YouTube.

- Practice one form of Listening to God through Scripture 2-3 times this week and journal about your experience

- Practice one form of Listening to God through Prayer 2-3 times this week and journal about your experience.

## Week 3
- Practice one form of Listening to God through Scripture 2-3 times this week and journal about your experience.

- Practice one form of Listening to God through Prayer 2-3 times this week and journal about your experience.

## Week 4
- Practice one form of Listening to God through Scripture following your groups selected reading schedule. Journal about your experience.

- Practice one form of Listening to God through Prayer 2-3 times this week and journal about your experience.

- Spend at least 1 hour in your Mission Space praying and observing. If you have the opportunity, invite someone in the Mission Space to try one of the Listening to God through Scripture and/or Prayer exercises. Journal about your experience.

## Articles

*Identity in Christ by S. Shaffer*

*New Identity Worksheet by S. Shaffer*

*Listening to God through Prayer by S. Carrizal*

*Reading Passages*

*Reflection Questions*

# Month 3
# Listening to God Through Mission

## Week 1
- Continue to practice Listening to God through Scripture and Prayer several times per week using your cohort's reading schedule.
- Read Listening to God through Mission by L. Howard and S. Shaffer.
- Make a plan to work on at least one mission direction.

## Week 2
- Continue your Listening to God through Scripture and Prayer rhythms.
- Practice one NEW form of Listening to God through Mission.
- Journal about your experiences.

## Week 3
- Continue your Listening to God through Scripture and Prayer rhythms.
- Practice one NEW forms of Listening to God through Mission.
- Journal about your experiences.

## Week 4
- Continue your Listening to God through Scripture and Prayer rhythms.
- Practice one NEW form of Listening to God through Mission.
- Journal about your experiences.
- Plan and take a 2–4-hour Silence and Solitude Retreat.

## Articles

# Month 4
# Balanced Life

## Week 1

- Continue to practice Listening to God through Scripture, Prayer, and Mission using your personal plan or a group schedule.

- Read Yielding to God by J. Hoover.

## Week 2

- Continue to practice Listening to God through Scripture, Prayer, and Mission using your personal plan or a group schedule.

- Create a personal disciplines rhythm that incorporates Listening to God via Scripture, Prayer, and Mission that you will commit to practicing.

## Week 3

- Continue to practice Listening to God through Scripture, Prayer, and Mission using your personal plan or a group schedule.

## Week 4

- Continue to practice Listening to God through Scripture, Prayer, and Mission using your personal plan or a group schedule.

- Reflect on your Discipleship Cohort journey.

## Articles

*Yielding to God – J. Hoover*

*Reflecting on your Discipleship Cohort Journey*

*Reflection Questions*

# What Is a Discipleship Cohort?

A discipleship cohort is a vehicle for Christians who want to learn, practice, and process what it means to participate in God's work in this world by listening to God and following His call.

What this group is:

**Rhythmic Ritual**: It is important to create a regular, set-apart, sacred time to meet as a community. This weekly meeting time is foundational to the DC and formative in each disciple's development.

**Push & Pull**: The DC is a space that features both encouragement and accountability. You will find the DC as an environment of grace, acceptance, support, and love, as well as one that encourages you to stretch, walk the extra mile, and keep the commitments you have made to the Lord, yourself, and this group.

**Mustard Seed Mentality**: The DC only consists of 4–6 participants because it is through small numbers of dedicated disciples that large movements will emerge. This community is about long-term growth over short-term success, systemic transformation over external veneer, and Kingdom expansion over Kingdom building.

**In the Trenches Leadership**: The DC facilitator is someone who has gone through an initial DC and has been trained to help cohorts joyously journey forward in an authentic and encouraging environment.

**Conversational & Confidential**: What happens in the DC stays in the DC, which should encourage you to be transparent, open, and honest about your life and ministry. We are all fellow travelers on the same road, so we all share some of the same burdens and challenges.

**Relational & Relaxed**: The DC is not designed as a classroom experience where the teacher teaches, and the students listen and learn. We all come to the group, not as empty vessels, but as people with knowledge, experience, and expertise led by the Spirit. The group is structured in a way that encourages you to share what you have and what God is doing in your life with the others.

**A Lived Faith**: The DC has a high view of Scripture and theological education but also holds to the premise that nothing is fully understood until it is practiced and passed on to others. The two questions that guide every session of the DC are: (1) What is God saying to me? (2) What am I going to do about it? These questions lay the foundation of everything we talk about in the group.

**4-Month Season**: The DC will meet (almost) every week for the duration of four months. This enables enough time to develop a balanced discipleship rhythm and habit, while keeping the time frame short enough for the rhythm not to become confining and monotonous.

**Exponential Multiplication**: The goal of the initial 16-week DC is to forge healthy rhythms that then expand in your local context by each participant being trained as a DC leader who gathers new groups. In addition, once groups complete the initial 16-week journey, they can apply the DC rhythms of listening to God through scripture, prayer, and mission as the basis of a long-term community dedicated to growing in Christ and participating in God's mission.

# Perspectives on Discipleship

*By Stephen Shaffer*

As we begin this journey together in a Discipleship Cohort, we want to share some of our perspectives on the nature and purpose of being disciples.

**Perspective #1 – Discipleship means participating in God's mission to restore all things.**

Steven Covey famously said, "begin with the end in mind" to highlight the importance of knowing the goal of your efforts. If we have the wrong idea about the "end," our efforts will be spent on the wrong things. This seems to be the case with Jesus' first disciples. When he first called those disciples, saying, "Come and follow me and I will make you fishers of men" (Matt 4:19; Mk 1:17) I think they had a different "end" in mind. They thought that Jesus was going to reestablish the kingdom of Israel the way it was under King David. Even after Jesus' resurrection, we hear the disciples ask, "Are you going to establish the kingdom now?" (Acts 1).

As the story of Acts unfolds, the disciples gain a clearer and clearer understanding of Jesus' mission and their participation in that mission. By Acts 3:21, Peter can declare, "He (Jesus) must remain in heaven until the time comes for God to restore everything, as he promised long ago through his holy prophets." In God's mind, the "end" is the restoration of all things, not just the restoration of Israel. Paul helps us to understand that Jesus' resurrection marks the beginning of a restoration that will not be fully realized until Jesus' second coming. With Jesus' resurrection, creation entered a new era, a new age of existence. In this new era, the followers of Jesus have the benefit of God's Holy Spirit as a guide and power to participate in God's work to restore all things.

With the clarity of God's end in mind, we ask the question, "What does the restoration of all things look like between now and Jesus' second coming?" For the answer to that question, we return to the ministry of Jesus. Jesus never describes in detail everything that might be involved with restoration; instead, he turns to the words of Isaiah to paint a picture of what it looks like, saying:

"The Spirit of the Lord is on me,

because he has anointed me

to preach good news to the poor.

He has sent me to proclaim freedom for the prisoners

and recovery of sight for the blind,

to release the oppressed,

to proclaim the year of the Lord's favor." (Isa 61:1–2; Lk 4:18–19, NIV)

The restoration movement of Jesus involves reversing Sin's attempts to impoverish, imprison, oppress, disfigure, divide, and kill to the extent made possible by the Spirit. So, we begin our journey as disciples with God's end "to restore all things" as our purpose.

**Perspective #2 – Discipleship involves increasingly yielding our life to God's purposes.**

If discipleship is participating in God's work to restore all things, then our question needs to be, "How do we participate in that purpose?" When Jesus prays, "Father if you are willing take this cup from me; yet not my will, but yours be done," (Lk 22:42, NIV) he expresses the central challenge we face as disciples—the challenge of yielding our will over to our Father's.

According to Romans 8, God has freed us from the power of Sin and inevitable death and given us His Spirit and the promise of Life. We now look forward to our own resurrection to eternal life and sharing in the glory of Christ. The presence of God's Spirit in us empowers us to resist temptations and distractions, assures us of our future hope, and helps us to know how to participate in God's work. But the gift of the Spirit does not magically change us in an instant. Instead, when we commit our life to Jesus, we begin a process of transformation empowered by that Spirit. At its core, that process involves (1) learning to understand God's will and (2) acting on that understanding by yielding our will to God's will. For us to say, "not my will but yours be done," we must understand God's will and learn to yield to it.

**Perspective #3 – Discipleship involves God's power combined with our intentional efforts.**

Romans 12:1–2 says that our transformation is a partnership between us and God. God actually does the transformation in us as we voluntarily submit to His will. As we yield, he transforms, and we grow. This progressive process allows us to grow in our understanding of God's will. The more we yield, the more we align and understand. It is important that we remember that we cannot defeat sin in our lives. If we could, we would not need the Spirit, and "Christ died for nothing" (Gal 2:21). Our role in transformation is submitting to God, allowing Him to change us into instruments for his purposes. To be intentional about yielding, we will need to develop intentional habits and rhythms that give God the opportunity to change us.

**Perspective #4 – Discipleship involves learning to listen to God and then acting on what we hear.**

In our Catalyze Coach training, we use a growth model we call the GEAR model of growth. The model asserts that our plans, decisions, and goals all flow out of our beliefs, values, and motives (BVM). Every goal we pursue, decision we make, and plan we pen flows from our conscious and subconscious BVM. When we put those plans and decisions into action, we will

inevitably discover that some things go as expected while other things do not. That gives us an opportunity to change our plans mid-course based on what we learn (ASSESS), and then at some point, we can look back on the whole situation (REFLECT) and modify our BVM based on what we have learned. The GEAR model assumes that growth is the process of changing our beliefs, values, and motives. Applying the GEAR model to discipleship, we can say the following:

Spiritual growth is a process that transforms our BVM so that they increasingly align with God's.

There the transformation of our BVM may occur before, during, or after we act:

> We may know God's will in a situation before we take action so that our plans are anchored in God's will from the start.

> We may come to a better understanding of God's will in the process of pursuing a particular direction and learn to yield along the way (ASSESS).

> We may come to an understanding of God's will only after the fact (REFLECT).

Over time, with continued discernment before we act, sensitivity in process, and reflection after the fact, we will progressively be transformed as we yield more and more of our will and energies into God's hands for His purposes. Spiritual growth requires a combination of discernment before, sensitivity during, and reflection after the fact. Another word for discernment, sensitivity, and reflection is *listening*. Discipleship is learning to listen to God and then acting on what we hear. Listening to God means attending to the work of the Spirit in us, for the Spirit is given to guide and empower us to do God's will.

Learning to listen to God involves more than reading to discover dos and don'ts and more than mere knowledge about God. We can read Scripture to discover that murder is a sin, but we cannot find in Scripture how our career fits into God's purposes. We cannot simply turn to a verse and discover all that God wants to send us to help a person in need. But we believe that God is not silent on these matters, that he desires to reveal His will to us, and he works powerfully in this world through disciples who yield to His leading.

We believe that there are habits and rhythms that help us attend to God's leading—that we can listen to God via Scripture, via prayer, via community, and via engaging in His mission.

**Listening via Scripture** – learning to let Scripture come alive in the moment and be more than knowledge.

**Listening via Prayer** – learning to leave space for God to speak, be silent, or quiet our own anxious spirit.

**Listening via Community** – learning to allow God to speak to us through trusted friends in relationship with us.

**Listening via Mission** – learning to discover Jesus in the people we serve and in the act of service.

As we learn to listen to God's voice, he leads us to lay down our lives more and more for the sake of His mission. In that process, we may yield our own desires, but we will surely find true life. "For whoever loses his life for my sake will find it."

# Commitment Pledge

**Motivation**- I will be driven first by my desire to be a disciple of Jesus and then to make disciples (in that order).

**Responsibility**- I will take responsibility for my own learning and be self-motivated to prepare for each week's cohort.

**Experience**- I will generously share my experience and knowledge with the group and will be an active participant in the discussions.

**Stick-to-itiveness**- I will make this group a priority in my life and not allow the constant demands for our time to interfere with my involvement.

**Context**- I will understand and appreciate I come from a unique context with a unique history and set of issues and will not merely take the information shared in the group and implement the DC content without first thinking through it contextually.

**Commitment**- I am willing to do the work, pay the fee, show up on time, and communicate with the facilitator and the group if life circumstances change or if I have questions, comments, or complaints.

**Multiplication**- I understand that the goal is to multiply what I have learned and experienced in this DC by starting a discipleship group of my own.

# Spiritual Journey Timeline Template

The goal of this exercise is to create a graph of your spiritual journey mapping its highs and lows over time.

Take a clean sheet of paper and hold it so it is wider than it is tall.

Mark a Center Line horizontally across the center of the page (label the line "Time").

Starting from the left (early in life), graph your spiritual journey as a line that rises and falls over time. Rising above the center line indicates a time when you felt particularly strong/close to God; falling below the center line indicates a time when you felt low/estranged from God.

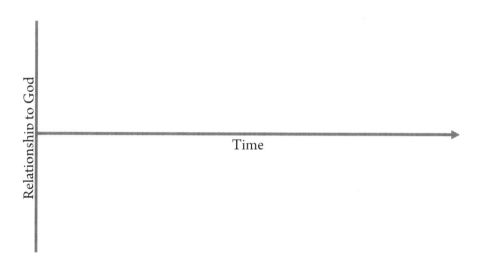

# Listening for God's Voice

*By Stephen Shaffer*

Learning to listen to God and attend to the Spirit will involve intentional habits and skills. Our goal is to follow a wisdom greater than our own as we progressively yield our life into God's hands for his purposes; to let His will be done. Learning to listen to God involves more than reading to discover dos and don'ts and more than mere knowledge *about* God. We believe that God is always acting in the world around us, and he often chooses to work through us as a means of advancing His kingdom. But he can only work through us if we are paying attention to His voice and are willing to yield.

Learning to listen to God through scripture, prayer, and mission involves strengthening spiritual disciplines and habits that help us pay attention and sift through what we experience. While there is no real formula for this process, there are some practices we can follow that will help us to be intentional.

## Pay Attention

The first step to listening is simply paying attention. We must first notice God at work. If, as we have said, God is at work in the world and desires that we join His efforts, then there are many opportunities for us to attend and pay attention to God. Sure, God could get our attention with something dramatic that we cannot ignore, but he often prefers to work through a "gentle whisper" (1 Kings 19:12, NIV). We are looking for that little something, a gentle nudge that gets our attention, an "aha," "hmm," or "wow." It could be a new insight from scripture, a nagging question, an unusual sense of peace, a persistently unsettled spirit, or a sense of wonder and awe. Sometimes, things will happen in life that appear as "open doors" or "closed doors." Not everything will be "the voice of God," but whatever it is that catches our attention, we want to pay attention and sift through it to discern God's presence.

## What is God saying?

After paying attention and noticing, we need to repeatedly ask ourselves: What is God saying?[1] This is where we need to slow down, pray, sift, and explore.

**Pray** – Take whatever you noticed—your "aha" "hmm" or "wow"—and discuss it with God in prayer, asking Him for insight and clarity. Prayerfully describe to God what you noticed, how it is affecting you, what you are curious about, the questions it raises, etc. Engage in conversation with God leaving plenty of silence for His Spirit to move within your heart and mind. Sit with Him, talk, listen, discuss, ask, seek, and knock. We believe that God wants us to know His will and has promised to answer, in His own time and His own way.

**Sift** – Sifting through the "aha" involves sorting out the difference between our will and God's will, our spirit and God's Spirit. Just because something gets our attention, and we have an "aha" moment does not mean that it is God who is behind it. Jesus prayed in the Garden, "not my will but yours" (Matt 26:42, NIV). To be about God's business, we must learn to tell the difference between our own will and God's will, our spirit and the Spirit. Elijah the prophet had to learn to recognize God's voice from among the other (and often louder) voices.

> The LORD said, "Go out and stand on the mountain in the presence of the LORD, for the LORD is about to pass by." Then a great and powerful wind tore the mountains apart and shattered the rocks before the LORD, but the LORD was not in the wind. After the wind there was an earthquake, but the LORD was not in the earthquake. After the earthquake came a fire, but the LORD was not in the fire. And after the fire came a gentle whisper. When Elijah heard it, he pulled his cloak over his face and went out and stood at the mouth of the cave. (1 Kings 19:11–13, NIV)

Sifting through to find God's voice involves learning to sift out the wind, earthquakes, and fires that seem like God's voice. God does indeed open some doors; others are simply the result of circumstances and the actions of others. Likewise, God closes some doors, while others are closed by changing circumstances or the will of others. When we experience an opportunity or an open door that is attractive, there is a temptation to think that God is blessing us with what we want. He might be or perhaps we are hearing the voice of our own will and spirit, not God's. Likewise, some closed doors or challenges we experience may be God trying to get us to rethink things, or it may simply be that the path is steep, and we need to press on. Just because something seems to "make sense" to us does not mean it is God; it may simply be our own thinking and interests speaking.

Sifting through these questions must begin with our inner commitment to indifference.[2] Indifference does not mean that we do not care. It means that we are open to whatever God wants. We do not have an opinion, idea, preference, or want other than what God wants. Of course, we will have opinions, ideas, and preferences, but for the sake of following God, we recognize them as our preferences and intentionally set them aside to give priority to doing God's will. "Not my will but yours." From this place of indifference, God can lead us into his will, and that is our greatest joy.

Explore – Like sifting and praying, exploring involves a willingness to hold the question of "what is God saying" open while we allow God to reveal his will. We actively resist the urge to jump to conclusions and assign a meaning until we have prayed, sifted, and explored. Exploring may involve asking faithful friends to pray and listen for God's voice with us. We may invite our discipleship cohort to ask us open questions that help us look at the topic in new ways. In this process, our goal is to remain open, committed, and willing to pursue *whatever* God reveals. During this exploration, we may experience a sense of peace and alignment that tells us we are in tune with God, or we may experience an unsettled spirit that tells us to keep praying, sifting, and exploring. God will lead us forward and reveal His will if we are patient about the process.

## What am I going to do about it?

After taking the time to explore if God was speaking and to ponder what He was saying, we must turn our attention to acting. If we, by faith, believe we have come to an understanding of God's will, then we, by

29

faith, need to do something about it. This is where we plan specific actions and organize our life around our new understanding of God's will. Sometimes this will mean pursuing significant changes in our life: a new career path, relocation, launching a project, etc. Other times it will mean less dramatic shifts in priorities, adding something to our efforts, stopping/starting a new habit, etc. Whatever it is, it is important that we take actions. Our plans and actions are also part of the way God reveals his will, and we need to reflect along the way, allowing God to reveal more of his will through our plans and actions. It is possible that we are unable to see God's entire path from where we begin the journey. So, he leads us to a new place, not as a destination but as a place where we gain a new perspective that opens further insights into His will. With every segment of the journey, God is leading, and our job is to pay attention, discern his voice, and move forward.

# Sanctification: Self-Control or Spirit-Control?

*By Tod Vogt*

> *No matter how much control we have over our lives,
> we find it hard to give it up. We can always find
> reasons to insist that we alone know what is best for
> ourselves. We are happy to accept suggestions from
> God, of course. We respect Christ greatly. But we
> reserve to ourselves the right to make the final
> decision[3]. — Keith Beasley-Topliffe*

God created each of us, and God has been pursuing each of us our entire life. While we describe our role in our salvation as 'coming to Christ' or 'accepting Christ' or 'making a decision for Christ,' the truth is, at best we gave-up our attempts to flee from God. These descriptions of our role place the initiative on us instead of on God.

> *The initiative is always God's. God laid claim to us
> long before we accepted that claim[4].*

It was not our pursuit of God but God's pursuit of us that leads to our salvation.

While we can accept that our eternal salvation is a gift of God and not by works, we frequently pursue spiritual growth by purely human effort. To believe that God worked to draw us to himself initially is one thing. It is something else altogether to believe that (and even more … to live as if) God is still working in the daily, moment-by-moment circumstances of life. We trust God with our eternity but not necessarily with our daily discipleship (sanctification).

Take for example how we frequently attempt to embody the Fruit of the Spirit in Galatians:

> *But the fruit of the Spirit is love, joy, peace,
> forbearance, kindness, goodness, faithfulness,
> gentleness and self-control. Against such things there
> is no law. (Gal 5:22–23, NIV)*

31

Many of us read this passage and conclude that the Apostle Paul is challenging us to exercise a greater degree of self-discipline, as if trying harder to love is the way we grow in love (vs 22). Is that the message? Is he encouraging the early Christians to better demonstrate peace (vs 22) by trying harder to be peaceful?

If that is the case, then the *acts of the flesh* mentioned in the preceding verses can be overcome by simply stopping them.

> *The acts of the flesh are obvious: sexual immorality,*
> *impurity and debauchery; idolatry and witchcraft;*
> *hatred, discord, jealousy, fits of rage, selfish*
> *ambition, dissensions, factions and envy;*
> *drunkenness, orgies, and the like. I warn you, as I did*
> *before, that those who live like this will not inherit*
> *the kingdom of God. (Gal 5:19–21, NIV)*

Is sexual immorality (vs 19) your sin? Stop it! Is jealousy (vs 20) your sin? Just stop being jealous! Is selfish ambition or envy or drunkenness (vss 20 & 21) your sin? Just stop being those ways! While the prevailing, common-sense advice may be to simply work harder or do better, this is not what the Apostle Paul writes. Merely exercising greater self-control is the opposite of what the Apostle Paul intends. The apostle's answer to *the acts of the flesh* (vs 19) is to *walk by the Spirit* (vs 16) or in verse 25:

> *Since we live by the Spirit, let us keep in step with*
> *the Spirit. (Gal 5:25, NIV)*

In short, the Apostle Paul suggest that the pathway to resisting the *flesh with its passions and desires* is not self-control but Spirit-control. Of course, that begs the question, 'What is Spirit-control?'

In Romans 8, the Apostle Paul describes two mutually exclusive realms of authority from which each believer lives. Each of us lives subject to either *the sinful nature* or *the Spirit*. The apostle describes these realms in totality, suggesting that one does not live partly in one and partly in the other.

In Romans 8:5–8 the apostle uses the language of 'the mind' as in, "*have their minds set on what the flesh desires*" (Rom 8:5, NIV) or "*the mind* governed by the Spirit is life and peace" (Rom 8:6, NIV). This comes from the Greek word *Phronêma* which describes the settled way we look at the world or, more commonly, 'mindset'. The apostle contrasts having a mindset rooted in *the flesh* with a mindset rooted in *the Spirit*. Our actions, then, are either motivated by a view of the world rooted in *what the flesh desires* or a view of the world rooted in *what the Spirit desires*.

Viewing the world through the lens of *what the Spirit* desires or exercising 'Spirit-control' happens by submission. We surrender viewing the world in ways that serve ourselves and surrender to a Spirit-governed view of the world. This is what the Apostle Paul imagines when he writes in Romans 12:1–2:

> *Therefore, I urge you, brothers and sisters, in view of God's mercy, to offer your bodies as a living sacrifice, holy and pleasing to God—this is your true and proper worship. Do not conform to the pattern of this world, but be transformed by the renewing of your mind. Then you will be able to test and approve what God's will is—his good, pleasing and perfect will. (Rom 12:1–2, NIV)*

The mind rooted in the flesh views the world in terms of self and acts accordingly. The self may be one's life, family, race, gender, nationality, denomination, political orientation, or any identity that reinforces the self and what the self desires. Conversely, the mind rooted in the Spirit views the world considering God and his purposes. When the disciple sets aside the mind governed by flesh and self and adopts the mind of the Spirit, actions change. The disciple no longer acts in ways to pursue what the self (in any of its manifestations) desires but acts in ways to pursue God's purposes.

Even when we start with *the mind of the Spirit*, we may find that we slip back into acting out of our *mind of the flesh*. This is at the core of the Apostle Paul's reproach of the Galatian disciples in Galatians 3:3:

> *After beginning by means of the Spirit, are you now trying to finish by means of the flesh? (Gal 3:3, NIV)*

Here we find ourselves back at the beginning. We may trust God with our eternal salvation (i.e., *beginning*) but then try to achieve sanctification (i.e., *trying to finish*) on our own. Our transformation comes from our surrender to the mindset of the Spirit as much as our salvation comes from God's grace. The more we remember that we are already secure in God's favor, the more we are free to act accordingly. Discipleship, then, is the progressive surrendering to the *mind of the Spirit* and acting out of that mind. The more we yield, the more we become attuned to the Spirit and the more aligned our actions are with God's intent in the world. Simply put, our discipleship relies more on submission than obedience.

## Spirit-Self Reflection Questions

In what ways do I need to rely on the Spirit more for transformation?

Why do I resist submitting to the Spirit?

How would my life be different if I focused on submission versus obedience?

What behaviors are not aligned with my new identity in Christ?

Where do I sense that the Spirit is leading me?

Why do I rely upon my own ability to grow and change?

What would I have to change to "set my mind" on the Spirit more often?

In what circumstances am I not allowing the Spirit to lead?

Why am I hesitant to let the Spirit lead?

# God Speaks: Listening to God Through Scripture

*By Steven Carrizal*

I have a friend who reads the Bible a lot. In fact, he told me once that he reads the Bible too much. Not sure how one could read the Bible too much, I asked him to explain. So, he clarified that maybe "too much" is not the best way to say it. Rather, he means that in his reading, he can over focus on Hebrew words or other research—as if the Bible were a history puzzle. He calls these pursuits "rabbit trails that really don't impact life"—trails that cause him to "miss the message God has put simply right in front of me."

My friend has a point. There are many interesting things in the Bible to distract an inquiring mind: words, customs, events, doctrine, and theology. Diving into these topics may satisfy our curiosity and bring clarity to our thinking. However, as with my friend, sometimes we can spend "so much time and energy on all the ways the word 'neighbor' was used two thousand years ago that I don't have the time or energy to actually get off my butt and help my neighbor who is in need." My friend has a point here, too. After all, it is the wise response after hearing the words of scripture (see Matthew 7:24–27). So, it might seem that the faithful pattern is to read, then do—hear the word, obey the word. Before we rush to this conclusion, let's not assume we know what God's desired action is for us and find ourselves in the identifying with the Pharisees. For all their efforts in searching the Scriptures and doing everything they found, they still failed to "come to Jesus" (John 5:39).

So maybe we encourage a moment of pause. Somewhere in between reading and doing, between inaction and reaction, we stop and listen. We want to make space for God to speak to us, and in that speaking, guide us—not only toward action, but even more toward awareness of the work of the Spirit in us and through us. What this requires from us is a different posture than we may be used to. Instead of quickly referencing connected passages or digging through reference guides (commentaries, lexicons, and dictionaries), we need to give scripture space. We change our role from explorer or researcher to listener. We slow down, sit back, soak in the words, and become open to the nudge of the Spirit.

Here are four ways of listening to God through Scripture.

## Lectio Divina

Contemplative in nature, this ancient way of attending to Scripture brings together reading and meditation. In a culture of information, consumption, speed, and efficiency, *lectio divina* can be a welcomed respite, a rest stop in midst of a busy day. *Lectio divina* won't get us through the Bible in a year, and it won't satisfy the need to pursue knowledge. Rather, this practice asks us to patiently wait and listen.

In his book *Finding Sanctuary*, Abbot Christopher Jamison says *lectio divina* helps us in three ways. First, we see the words before us "as a gift to be received, not a problem to be dissected."[5] Rather than bringing our questions to the passage, we let the words question us. Second, *lectio* is slow and repetitive. This is not a quick read. Each pass through the text is deliberate and thoughtful. Third, the whole process flows out of prayer and leads us through prayer. The words on the page move into our hearts and shape the words of our prayer.

One of the beauties of lectio divina is its flexibility and portability. It can be practiced alone or with others and the length of time needed for it depends on the length of the text and time given for silence and journaling/sharing. Here's a basic format:

Start with a time of silence.

First Pass: Read the passage slowly listening for a word, phrase, or image from the text that stands out. Sit in silent reflection on that word, phrase, or image. Listen for and receive anything you may hear God saying to you though this text. Write down or share this word, phrase, or image.

Second Pass: Read the passage again. This time imagine yourself in the setting. What do you see, sense, or experience? Sit in silent refection with this new layer of imagination. Listen for and receive anything you may hear God saying to you though this text. Write down or share how the text opens up in your imagination.

Third Pass: Read the passage a third time. This time notice any comfort or discomfort you may be feeling. Sit in silent reflection on how God is working in you through this text. What is God calling you to do or not do, to pick up or lay down? Write down or share how you feel called to respond.

Finish with a time of silence.

## Dwelling in the Word[6]

Dwelling in the Word is a modern adaptation of *lectio divina* that invites people to listen to scripture, to God, and to one another. While it shares some characteristics, like slow repetitive reading and reflection, it differs in two particular ways. One difference is that it is intended to be communal exercise in which people listen attentively to one another. Another difference is that the group doing the "dwelling" returns to the same passage for a long period of time, even a year or two. Developed as a method for congregations to discern how God is calling them into missional action, Dwelling in the Word has become an exercise for any kind of group (large or small) desiring to use scripture as a way to discern what God is doing in and through them.

A session of Dwelling in the Word for a small group looks something like this:

Start with a time of silence.

Read the selected passage. Participants listen for a verse, phrase, or word that stands out. Everyone sits in time of silent reflection.

Following this reflective move, the group moves to sharing and listening. Each person has the opportunity to briefly share what stood out from this reading of the passage and something which they would like to learn more about. While one person is sharing, all others are listening deeply to the one sharing. In the practice of Dwelling in the Word, this is called "listening the other into free speech" as the rest of the group creates a safe place for the sharing.

In the last move of this exercise, each member of the group retells what another group member said. This is done around the circle until everyone has shared and everyone has been repeated.

Dwelling in the Word is a practice that opens us up not only to what God may be saying to us, but more importantly, how God is moving in the mind and heart of another person. This requires a different kind of attentiveness than just processing our own reflections.

## Three Column Bible Study (Adapted for a Listening Exercise)

The three-column method is an inductive approach to Bible study. However, with some adaptations, it can be very useful as a listening exercise individually and with small groups. As with *lectio divina* and Dwelling in the Word, start with a passage that is no more than eight to ten verses. Next, take a regular sheet of paper, turn it to the landscape orientation, and divide it into three columns. In the first column, write the passage word for word. Doing so requires deliberate attention to each word forcing you to go slow. Follow this step with a period of silence. Let the words that you just wrote settle into your heart. Listen for the message of the passage to come through. Then, in the second column, rewrite the passage in your own words. Do your best Eugene Peterson imitation, summarize the passage, or write as if for young children to understand. Follow this step with another period of silence. Where do you feel the nudge of the Spirit? What do you hear God saying to you? If you are with a group, take a moment to share summaries before entering the silence. In the third column, write down "This is what I hear" statements. This is a great place to answer the question "What am I hearing from God and how do I respond?" Again, if you are with a group, take a moment to share responses.

## On Location

One of the most creative ways to listen to God through scripture is to read the Bible on location and with unlikely reading partners. In other words, get out of the comfortable setting of the study, the living room, or the classroom. In his book *Reading the Bible with the Damned*, Bob Ekblad says that a change in scenery can help us with a change in perspective. He calls for taking the Bible to the streets, to the prisons, to the slums. Read the Gospels with today's tax collectors and sinners.

Read the Exodus story with today's slaves. Find the addicted, the undocumented, the disabled, and the ex-con. Use any of the three listening practices above and consider these questions: How does a new context change what you hear in the passage? What do these new reading partners hear in the passage that you haven't? Take notes and listen for what God is saying to you through scripture as experienced in the lives of those marginalized in our world.

## Conclusion

If you are like me and from a church tradition that highly values the Bible, then Bible study has been a priority. It's what we do in our class times, in our small group times, and in our quiet times. We have been trained to have an unquenchable thirst for knowledge gained from the Bible. The exercises above offer a different approach, unfamiliar and uncomfortable. They are about giving scripture space to read us, for the Spirit to speak to us, for God to call forth from us the Jesus life. Rest in the word and listen.

# Adopting a Mission Space

The life of a disciple involves living in relationship to God, to one another, and reaching out to the world around us. To live a balanced life as a disciple, we need to be intentional about all three dimensions. In general terms, we tend to be good at enjoying our relationships with one another, work at spending regular time with God, but have limited experience building relationships with those outside Christ to continue the mission. During the course of this Discipleship Cohort, you will be challenged to strengthen your discipleship by investing in all three dimensions. To strengthen the out dimension, you will be asked to adopt a mission space.

A mission space is any public space where you can spend time, encounter others, and look for God's activity. It can be a park, coffee shop, pub, shopping center, neighborhood, restaurant, library, or just about anywhere. The goal is to choose a place, spend time there often so that it is familiar to you, and you become a familiar part of the space to others. You will spend time there, praying for and in the space, listen to what is going on, and observe the movements of people and more importantly observe God's activity there. You may meet new people, engage in simple conversations, show hospitality, experience the generosity of others. We have come to believe that God is at work in people and places all around us in ways that we often ignore or overlook. So, we want to learn to pay attention and attend to God's movement looking for ways to join Him in His work.

## Choosing a space:

The idea is simply to select a public space that you can visit often and spend time getting to know the place and people. Consider the following as you make your selection:

- It should be someplace that you visit in the normal course of life. Not necessarily a place you visit often, but at least a place that you have a reason to be there. Pick a place you enjoy, a place where you already spend time, a place that is comfortable and fits you.

- It should be a place where you will encounter other people. It does not have to be a busy place, but it should not be a place of solitude.

- You will be spending time in the space—walking, working, sitting, praying, listening, conversing, watching.

- Pray about your options, listen for God's leading, and be thoughtful but don't overthink it.

- Ideas for places include a coffee shop, pub, park, neighborhood, restaurant, shopping center, mall, gym, recreation center, community center, or library.

## Adopt and Pay Attention:

- Each month you will be asked to spend time in your adopted mission space. Your goal is to make the space part of your life and pay attention—observing, listening, visiting, praying, and enjoying the people that are there.

- Over the course of time, you will probably see some of the same people—the employees, cashiers, baristas, neighbors, and others who enjoy the space. Take the opportunity to meet them and strike up a simple conversation. Get to know them, their situations, hopes, etc.

- Three Questions - One simple way to get to know people beyond a head nod or simple hello, is to think of three questions that get progressively more personal. For example: "How is your day going?", "What plans do you have for the summer?" "What are you looking forward to?" You are not trying to accomplish anything in particular, not trying to sell them something, convince them of anything, or invite them to something. You simply want to get to know them a little more.

- Pray regularly—for the space, place, and people. Ask God to reveal where he is at work, to give you eyes to see and ears to hear, and to open a door to relationship. Don't try to force it; just be present, intentional, and open.

# Listening to God Through Scripture Passages

## Suggested Individual Passages

<u>Old Testament</u>

    Exod 3:1–10

    1 Kings 19:9b–13

    Ezek 37:1–10; Ezek 47:1–12

    Psalm 23

    Psalms

<u>New Testament</u>

    Matthew 4:1–11; Matthew 5:1–10; Matthew 6:5–13

    Luke 4:14–21; Luke 10:1–12

    John 1:1–18

    Acts 3:1–10

    Romans 12:1–12

    1 Cor 2; 1 Cor 13:1–7; 1 Cor 9:19–23

    2 Cor 5:14–21

    Eph 3:14–21

    Phil 1:9–11; Phil 2:1–11

    Col 3:12–17

    2 Peter 1:3–11

    Heb 5:11–14

    1 John 4:1–6

# Group Reading Schedules

*These can be used in two different ways: (1) read the same passage every day or (2) read a different passage from the series each day.*

**Ephesians:** Eph 1:3–10; Eph 1:11–14; Eph 1:15–23; Eph 2:1–10; Eph 2:11–22; Eph 3:7–13; Eph 3:14–21

**Matthew**: Matt 6:5–15; Matt 6:16–18; Matt 6:19–24; Matt 6:25–34; Matt 7:1–6; Matt 7:7–12; Matt 7:15–23

**1 Peter:** 1 Pet 1:3–9; 1 Pet 1:10–12; 1 Pet 1:13–21; 1 Pet 1:22–2:3; 1 Pet 2:4–12; 1 Pet 2:13–17; 1 Pet 2:18–25

# Identity in Christ

*By Stephen Shaffer*

When I was younger, I enjoyed listening to the The Who's classic rock song which asks the question, "Who are you … I really wanna know." I think inside I was saying, "I really do want to know." In my naïve pursuits to discover who I was/am, I learned to play an identity game—a game where I earned labels based on my actions or attributes. When I played sports, I earned an "athletic" label. When I did well in school, I earned a "smart" label. I worked hard to get the labels I liked, and harder to avoid other labels. Later, I noticed that the rules were not always fair. Sometimes people gave me a label I didn't deserve or want. My dentist labeled me "*Schnoz*" because he thought I had a big nose. I also discovered that some labels were harder to change than others. I could lose the athletic label but couldn't lose the "chubby" label. I was playing the identity game long before I knew it was a game.

The identity game has two basic rules: the *action-identity* rule and the *label-identity* rule. The *action-identity* rule states that labels are earned on the basis of actions. Aristotle helped to make this a permanent rule in the identity game when he famously said, "We are what we repeatedly do." According to Aristotle, our actions define our identity. The *action-identity* rule seems inherently logical, fair, and offers me some control over my identity. If I repeatedly do athletics, act reliably, or help others, I should obtain those identity labels. It doesn't take long to learn that identity labels are not always fair. Sometimes I work very hard and never earn the label or I earn a label without ever doing anything. That's when we discover the second rule in the identity game, the *label-identity* rule.

The *label-identity* rule states that anyone can assign any label using any definition they choose. I receive the labels of fat, skinny, pretty, homely, arrogant, or athletic based on someone's assessment, opinion, or judgment. The definitions and the reasons vary from person to person. To some people, I am arrogant, to others wise. I have also discovered that I assign myself labels almost as indiscriminately as others. Despite the indiscriminate and illogical nature of these labels, we tend to believe them and allow them to shape our sense of identity.

The *action-identity* and *label-identity* rules define an identity game that shapes our perceptions and prevents us from realizing our full potential in Christ in at least three ways.

**The burden of change** – The *action-identity* rule places the burden of creating, sustaining, and changing our identity on us. Whether the name/label is something we want to shed or something we want to keep, we are the ones that will have to make it happen. The uncertainty of the *label-identity* rule undermines our ability to achieve our goal. The burden of constantly living up to expectations and overcoming perceptions is exhausting and even hopeless.

**The need to deceive** – In the process of trying to shed unwanted labels and earn those we desire, we encounter the disparity between how others perceive us (*label-identity*) and how we perceive ourselves (*label-identity*). Others may see us as confident, able, or generous while we feel insecure, unable, and stingy. Since we desire the confident label, we learn to fake confidence despite deep insecurities. We pretend we are fine, capable, and in-control despite being lonely, lost, and overwhelmed. The deception only traps us further in the identity game.

**The fear of insignificance** – Deep in our hearts, we all want to be significant. In the identity game, we often gauge significance by measuring ourselves against others. Sometimes we come out ahead, but more often, we are left with an enduring sense of being less than we want or less than others expect. There is always someone smarter, prettier, or more capable. There is always something we could have done or should have done. Furthermore, the rules of the game place the blame for this failure on us.

## Changing the rules

When we first come to Christ, the *action-identity* and *label-identity* rules are already deeply rooted. Although we know that something has changed, we continue to believe that God assigns the "Christian" label when we act in Christian ways (*action-identity*). The God assigned label is better than other labels, but it is still a label. The continued belief in the *action-identity* rule distorts grace into God grading on a curve, labelling us "good" (*label-identity*) so long as we do our best and try hard (*action-identity*). This is a partial conversion.

When we are in Christ, the rules change. Instead of us establishing our identity by our actions (*action-identity*), God gives us an identity as sons and daughters based on faith. Instead of the random labels based on the evaluations of self and others (*label-identity*), God declares us to be righteous.

## A New Identity - We ARE sons/daughters of God

In Christ, God gives us an identity on the basis of our faith, not action. If we are in Christ, we are sons and daughters—period. There are no additional identity-labels to pursue, and none that are available. We are children of God, adopted as Christ's brothers and sisters, and given an identity far beyond what we could ever have hoped to achieve by our own actions. Consider the following passages that affirm this idea:

"... to all who received him [Christ], to those who believed in his name, he gave the right (or power) to become children of God ..." (John 1:12, NIV)

"Spirit testifies with our spirits that we are children of God." (Rom 8:15, NIV)

"Now if we are children, then we are heirs—heirs of God and co-heirs with Christ, if indeed we share in his sufferings in order that we may also share in his glory. (Rom 8:17, NIV)

"But when the time had fully come, God sent his Son, born of a woman, born under law, to redeem those under law, that we might receive the full rights of sons. Because you are sons, God sent the Spirit of his Son into our hearts, the Spirit who calls out, 'Abba, Father.' So, you are no longer a slave, but a son; and since you are a son, God has made you also an heir. (Gal 4:4–6, NIV)

In Christ we are not simply *called* sons and daughters; we *are* sons and daughters of God with the full status as heirs. Adoption reverses the old *action-identity* rule. Instead of actions creating an identity, our identity shapes our actions. Since we are sons and daughters, God calls us to live in ways consistent with our identity. When we live out our identity in Christ, we reveal that it is Christ at work in us. This is expressed most clearly in the following,

"Follow God's example, therefore, as dearly loved children [2]and walk in the way of love, just as Christ loved us and gave himself up for us as a fragrant offering and sacrifice to God." (Eph 5:1-2, NIV)

"Since then, you have been raised with Christ, set your hearts on things above, where Christ is seated at the right hand of God. [2]Set your minds on things above, not on earthly things." (Col 3:1-2, NIV)

The Ephesian author says we should imitate God and walk in love as children, not to become children. The Colossian author tells us to think and act since we "have been raised" (past tense). God has given us a new identity and calls us to live consistent with who we already are. So, there is an expectation that our actions will change. To accept an identity as a son or daughter without yielding to God's transformation of our actions is also a failure to realize who we are in Christ. Grace should have an effect on our actions, but it flows from identity to action, not the reverse.

## A New Label - We ARE Righteous

In Christ, we are righteous on the basis of grace through faith, not actions. But our continued belief in the identity-game rules distorts the meaning of grace and hinders our maturity in Christ. Two common distortions of grace that I observe are checkbook grace and as-if grace.

### Checkbook grace

Despite knowing that our actions flow from our identity in Christ, we can continue to traffic in *action-identity*. Often, we would rather work for something than accept a hand-out, and at some level, grace feels like a hand-out. After all, we are generally good people and feel reasonably competent to manage our behaviors. We know we are not fully capable of doing everything right, but we are also not all bad. In this frame of mind, grace functions like overdraft protection on our checking account. Most of the time, we keep our account from going negative, but it's nice to know that if we run into trouble, our checks won't bounce. The remnants of the *action-identity* tease us into thinking that we are pretty good on our own, but it's nice to know that if we run into sin trouble, grace will cover us.

## As-if grace

Another distortion of grace is what I call as-if grace. As-if grace is when we think that grace is God grading us on a curve, treating us "as-if" we are righteous, even though we are not actually righteous. Scripture reveals that God does not treat us "as-if" we are righteous; he declares us righteous, not on the basis of our actions but on the basis of being in Christ. Let's look further into this.

> *"Therefore, since we have been made righteous*
> *through faith, we have peace with God through our*
> *Lord Jesus Christ, through whom we have gained*
> *access by faith into this grace in which we now stand."*
> *(Rom 5:1-2, NIV)*

If you read this verse in many modern English translations, you may see the word "justified" instead of the phrase "made righteous." In Greek, the word often translated "justified" is simply the verb form of the noun "righteous." English does not have a verb form for "righteous," forcing English translations to use a verb from a different root. Unfortunately, the choice of the verb "justified" does not convey the same meaning as "made righteous." I've heard teachers try to explain the meaning of justification using the phrase "just-as-if-I." God treats us as-if we are righteous. It is the as-if part of this definition that becomes the problem. To say that I AM righteous by faith is very different from saying God treats me *as if* I am righteous. Paul clearly says that we have been made righteous on the basis of faith. To say that God treats us "as if" we are righteous is to understand grace as God lowering his standards to accept us where we are and treating us as if we are what we are not. Romans tells us that instead of lowering his standards, God empowers us with the Holy Spirit to conquer sin and become the people He wants us to be. Romans 8:3–4 expresses this, saying:

> *"For what the law was powerless to do in that it was*
> *weakened by the sinful nature, God did by sending his*
> *own Son in the likeness of sinful man to be a sin*
> *offering. And so, he condemned sin in sinful man, [4] in*

49

*order that the righteous requirements of the law might
be fully met in us, who do not live according to the
sinful nature but according to the Spirit."*

The Law was simply a definition of what it means to be "good." While laws and definitions provide a way to measure "goodness," they don't provide any power to live up to the standards they express. Paul says that instead of changing His criteria, God gave us the ability to fully meet the righteous requirements of the law.

## True Discipleship

Discipleship is living as sons and daughters of God, rejecting the false identities associated with the *action-identity* or *label-identity* rules, and allowing the Holy Spirit to transform our weakness, freeing us to engage in our God-given roles within the kingdom. We are called to put forth effort, but our efforts should be focused on fully embracing who we are in Christ, not in *action-identity* or *label-identity* games. To perpetuate *action-identity* ideas will keep us from realizing the fullness of God's love, mercy, and grace and hinder our participation in God's work. Our new identity in Christ changes the game in three additional ways:

**The freedom to be honest** – Since our identity is given to us by God on the basis of faith and not the product of our actions, we are free to be honest with ourselves and others. When playing the *action-identity* game, we learned to deceive others and ourselves hiding our struggles, weakness, fears, anxieties, and sin. As sons and daughters, we are free to confess our sins, share our weaknesses, and express our anxieties with one another. When we are honest with God, ourselves, and others, the alienation that stems from deception is healed. Consequently, we find wholeness, integrity, authenticity, and peace.

**The power to be transformed** – Through that Spirit, God helps us defeat sin while he leads us to continue his mission through works of service. The essence of discipleship is expressed in Romans 8:12f where Paul says,

> *"Therefore, brothers and sisters, we have an
> obligation—but it is not to the flesh, to live according to*

*it. [13] For if you live according to the flesh, you will die; but if by the Spirit you put to death the misdeeds of the body, you will live, [14] because those who are led by the Spirit of God are sons of God. [15] For you did not receive a spirit that makes you a slave again to fear, but you received the Spirit of sonship. And by him we cry, 'Abba, Father.' [16] The Spirit himself testifies with our spirit that we are God's children. [17] Now if we are children, then we are heirs—heirs of God and co-heirs with Christ, if indeed we share in his sufferings in order that we may also share in his glory."*

The Holy Spirit is the power to defeat sin in our life. That power means that we don't have to discount the beauty of being human. We don't have to settle for being simply human; we are humans indwelt by the Holy Spirit, humans empowered to conquer sin.

**The opportunity to join God's mission** – Rather than a fear of insignificance, as God's children, we are partners with God in his business of reaching all humanity with a message of reconciliation. Consider the following:

"So, from now on we regard no one from a worldly point of view. Though we once regarded Christ in this way, we do so no longer. [17] Therefore, if anyone is in Christ, he is a new creation; the old has gone, the new has come! [18] All this is from God, who reconciled us to himself through Christ and gave us the ministry of reconciliation: [19] that God was reconciling the world to himself in Christ, not counting men's sins against them. And he has committed to us the message of reconciliation. [20] We are therefore Christ's ambassadors, as though God were making his appeal through us. We implore you on Christ's behalf: Be reconciled to God." (2 Cor 5:16–20, NIV)

"I no longer call you servants, because a servant does not know his master's business. Instead, I have called you friends, for everything that I learned from my Father I have made known to you. [16] You did not choose me, but I chose you and appointed you to go and bear fruit—fruit that will last. Then the Father will give you whatever you ask in my name." (John 15:15f, NIV)

God has declared us righteous by faith, given us a new identity as sons and daughters, empowered us with the Spirit, and granted us the opportunity to participate in his work. Now that is a new identity.

## Identity-Action Reflection Questions

How can I trust my "new heart" and "new Spirit" more?

What prevents me from claiming God's declaration of righteousness?

How can I create space in my day to connect more deeply with God?

What can I do to remind myself of who I am in Christ?

What would change if I relied more on the power of the Spirit to change me?

How do I try to maintain an identity in the eyes of others?

In what ways do I measure my worth by comparing myself to others (at home, at work, at church, within family)?

How would I complete the sentence: "I am significant because … "?

How would my treatment of others change if I believed that I am truly righteous?

If I fully claimed my identity in Christ, what would be different?

# New Identity Reflections Worksheet

Prayerfully consider each of the following areas and rate how significant each area is to your life and discipleship.

### The burden of change –

### The need to deceive –

### The fear of insignificance

# God Speaks: Listening to God Through Prayer

*By Steven Carrizal*

About midway through my college years, I met some people who lit my spiritual life on fire—or maybe I should say that God lit my spiritual life on fire through these new friends. The key practice they introduced to me was quiet time—morning time spent in Bible reading and prayer. It was the prayer part of this that sparked the fire. Growing up in a ministry family (my dad was a preacher), I was no stranger to prayer. I was surrounded by prayer—in church, at home, on vacation, in large groups, in small groups, and alone. People all around me modeled genuine, heartfelt prayer. Yet, in college, I experienced a more serious approach to prayer that was intentional and intense. I learned to present my life before God and plead for change, healing, and insight for myself and my friends. So, I kept a running list of people and specific circumstances to pray for. Each morning (well, most mornings), I faithfully named these in prayer. During this time, I found great purpose and expended much energy in the work of praying.

However, though my experience in college was transformative, through the years, I began to struggle with the growing list I was praying through. People shared difficult circumstances and deep suffering. I discovered that I did not have the capacity to maintain an emotional or compassionate connection to these situations. Eventually, I stopped praying through the list. Without a way to deepen the spiritual reservoir needed for such outpouring, I wore out and felt dry.

Then I got to know a woman in my church at the same time I began a graduate class on Spiritual Formation. While the spiritual formation class gave me the information, the woman in my church became my teacher. Both taught me something new about prayer—*to listen*. My practice of prayer until this point had always been about me speaking to God; no one taught me how to stop talking and, instead, rest in the presence of God. The more I learned to sit with God and listen, I discovered that the weight of my list floated away as I realized God already knew what was on it. Instead of doing all the speaking, I began to give space to the presence of God. I learned to sit in the quiet, to welcome the silence, to pay attention to the nudge of the Spirit, feel God's embrace, and listen to God's voice.

Prayer as listening does not replace prayer as speaking. Rather, it deepens and matures our relationship with God. Just as there is a rhythm in our personal relationships of speaking and listening, there are times to speak to God, but also times when I need to take the posture of Samuel—"Speak, Lord, for your servant is listening" (1 Samuel 3:9, NIV).

## Silence

Before any listening can happen in prayer, there must be silence. We need a nice quiet place free of external distractions. We also need to quiet our mind and heart to prepare "the way for inner seclusion and enables us to listen to the quiet voice of the Spirit."[7] We begin our listening in silence. But how do we nurture that silence? Here are some practices that open up that space to hear God speak.

## Breath Prayer

This is an important starting place for me. Breath prayer is the exercise that sparked my renewed life of prayer. In both Greek and Hebrew, the word for breath and spirit are the same. Breath prayer combines breath and spirit in the same moment so that our spirit is caught up with the Spirit of God as we breathe. In breath prayer, we find a sentence that heightens our awareness of who God is, how God is already at work, or connects with our need for God.[8] We then say the sentence in the rhythm of our breathing—first half as we inhale, second half as we exhale. In the process, we nurture the internal silence as the words become background to the presence of God.

Determine an amount of time for your exercise. For starters, set a timer for five minutes.

Identify a sentence from a passage. Again, for starters, use the opening sentence of Psalm 42: "As the deer pants for streams of water, so my soul pants for you, my God."

Start your time and breathe the sentence in and out: (inhale) *as the dear pants for streams of water;* (exhale) *so my soul pants for you, my God.*

At the end of the time, reflect on the brief exercise and write down your thoughts on one these questions: How did you experience the presence of God in this moment? How did this one sentence shape your perceptions of yourself, of God, and the life you are living?

## Listening List

Somewhat like a prayer list, which we might develop for intercessory prayer, a listening list details various concerns in our circle of influence. However, whereas in a prayer list we ask God for specific outcomes, with a listening list we lay the items one by one and ask what it is the Lord desires of us in each situation.

Come to the silence, creating a buffer from the previous moments of activity and the moments of prayer to come. Centering prayer is a good way to do this. Focus in on your breathing on some sacred word, phrase, or image that helps you put the world around us aside.

After a few minutes, look at your list. (This would work best with an abbreviated list—no more than five items.) In silence, slowly process your list in your mind, pausing as you read each item. Instead of requesting God's action, ask this: "Lord, how can I respond in this circumstance?" Sit with this question in silence for another minute or two.

Reflect on this experience. What do you sense God asking of you?

## Life-Centered Prayer[9]

Though we may try to hide from others and even ourselves, we cannot hide from God. *Examen* is a practice that helps us carry out the psalmist's prayer: "Search me, God, and know my heart; test me and know my anxious thoughts. See if there is any offensive way in me and lead me in the way everlasting" (Psalm 139:23–24, NIV). It is a practice of self-examination and awareness of our life, daily or weekly. It is an opportunity to lay ourselves open and let God identify what is happening, where we need confession, and where we need transformation. One way to do this is through an exercise called *Life-Centered Prayer*—a process of self-examination that takes place at the end of the day and takes into account the day's major events. The following is an adaptation for use in a group meeting.

*Gather*: Think through the highs and lows of the previous week and identify one event on which to focus. You might start with making a list in writing then circling the event of choice.

*Review*: As you focus on this one event, reflect upon it without judgement or excuses.

*Give thanks*: Consider how you can find gratitude in this event. Where was God present? How did God provide for or sustain you? Give thanks now for what you might have been unable to sense in the moment.

*Confess*: Consider any fault (thought, word, or deed) of yours in this event. Is there any wrong you recognize now for which you are responsible? Confess that sin.

*Find meaning*: Reflect on the significance of this event with questions such as, What is God saying to me? What am I being called to do? How is this connected to the rest of my life? Share something you sense God teaching you in this event.

## Ask the Heart[10]

This is another exercise of *Examen*. More than awareness, though, with this exercise we seek clarity around a particular issue. Here is the process:

Identify a specific question you want to explore. Here is one to try: Have I ever expected to hear God's voice? How would I know if I heard it?[11]

Start the process of silence by relaxing your body and mind. Breathe deeply.

As thoughts move to the side, think about the question slowly and gently. Savor each thought.

After a determined period of silence, bring your attention back to the present. Reflect on your experience and make note of what you learned by writing in a journal and/or sharing with a friend.

Here are other questions you might ask: Am I becoming less afraid of being known by God? Is prayer developing in me as a welcome discipline? Am I learning to move beyond personal offense and freely forgive those who have wronged me?[12]

## Conclusion

Listening to God in prayer does not come easy for those of us who are used to doing all the talking. We may struggle with staying focused in the silence, or we may struggle to know how God is speaking to us. Do not be disheartened. Though the exercises above may prove challenging at first, improvement comes with practice. Be patient, rest in the silence, and listen.

# Listening to God Through Mission

*By Lantz Howard & Stephen Shaffer*

Being a disciple means that we learn to listen to God and shape our lives around the will, purposes, and priorities of God for the sake of His mission. Just as God sent his Son into the world to demonstrate His love for us, Jesus sends us into the world to love the world for the sake of God's mission. We listen to God via prayer and Scripture to hear God's will for our life, to align our decisions and priorities to his purposes, and to progressively deepen our understanding of God and his unfathomable love for His creation. The more we know God, the more we think like God, the more we act in response to His call, the more we will discover the joy and abundance of being one with the Father and living for the sake of others. Our life as disciples is a long journey of transformation where we progressively deepen our understanding of God's will and increasingly yield to His plans and purposes.

Growing in our understanding of God must combine head and heart so that what we know intellectually shapes the wants and desires of our heart. Growing in our understanding of God must also involve action—putting our knowledge in motion. While our listening to God via Scripture and Prayer may spur us into action, our actions help us to see God in new ways. In the parable of the Sheep and Goats, Jesus says to those who fed the hungry, welcomed the strangers, clothed the needy, healed the sick, and visited the imprisoned—"whatever you did for one of the least of these brothers and sisters of mine, you did to me" (Matt 25:40, NIV). The wording is intentional; Jesus does not say that his followers did these actions *for* Jesus—the actions were done *to* Jesus. Somehow, by putting their faith into action, these followers encountered Jesus in the process. While they were feeding the hungry, taking care of the needy, and attending to the sick, they were deepening their interactions with Jesus Himself. Paul also reflects on the relationship between knowing and doing in his letter to the Philippians when he says,

> *"Not that I have already obtained all this, or have already arrived at my goal, but I press on to take hold of that for which Christ Jesus took hold of me. Brothers and sisters, I*

61

*do not consider myself yet to have taken hold of it. But
one thing I do: Forgetting what is behind and straining
toward what is ahead, I press on toward the goal to win
the prize for which God has called me heavenward in
Christ Jesus. All of us, then, who are mature should take
such a view of things. And if on some point you think
differently, that too God will make clear to you. Only let
us live up to what we have already attained."* (Phil 3:12–
16, NIV)

As we press on toward the goal of yielding our life to God, Paul says, "let
us live up to what we have already attained," or in other words, let's put
into action what we already understand. So, acting and engaging in
God's mission is another way of learning about God and listening to
God.

Listening to God through Mission begins with a recognition that we are
God's ambassadors seeking to share God's message of reconciliation as
Paul says,

*"So, from now on we regard no one from a worldly
point of view. Though we once regarded Christ in this
way, we do so no longer. Therefore, if anyone is in
Christ, the new creation has come: The old has gone,
the new is here! All this is from God, who reconciled us
to himself through Christ and gave us the ministry of
reconciliation: that God was reconciling the world to
himself in Christ, not counting people's sins against
them. And he has committed to us the message of
reconciliation. We are therefore Christ's ambassadors,
as though God were making his appeal through us."* (2
Cor 5:16–20, NIV)

As disciples, we are called to align our thought with God's thoughts,
align our will with God's will, align our behavior with God's ways, and
align our efforts with God's mission.

Like other areas of discipleship, taking up God's mission will mean
developing new habits and being intentional in our endeavors. Here are
several practical ways we can begin to listen to God through being on

mission. We are not looking to add evangelism tasks to our list but rather to adopt more natural lifestyle-based ways to build relationships and become involved in people's lives allowing God's presence in us to be a sign of God's love and a door to the possibility of faith.

## Marketplace Interactions

We interact with people every day as we go about our usual routines. A barista makes our custom coffee, someone helps us locate items in a store, cashiers tally our bill and bag our purchases, and servers bring our food and fill our glasses. We are surrounded by people doing their jobs. The problem is that many times we interact with people on a functional basis rather than as real people. We don't see the person; we see their function, and mostly their function is to make our experience in life better. When we are on mission, we see people, not functions. A barista doesn't brew our coffee; Bill does. Emma always has a smile as she scans my groceries. Take the opportunity of each of these interactions to get to know the people, learn their names, listen to their stories, recognize them, and be recognizable. Take the challenge to greet everyone you interact with, learn their names, use the three questions (mentioned in the Mission Space article), pray for them daily. In your prayers, ask God, "What do you want me to know/hear/learn from _____?"

## Hospitality

Hospitality means opening space in your life for others to be part of your world. In the narrow sense, it means having them over for a meal, but in the broader sense, it means treating others as if they were part of your family. It doesn't have to be a special occasion or a fancy event, just a time to share life which will almost always involve food. Lantz shares three examples of how his family has pursued the habit of hospitality.

As we looked at the social events our church had planned, I began to ask, "What if I started hosting this event at my house?" This question caused me to realize that many of my neighbors would never come to a church ice cream social or pancake breakfast, so instead of asking them to go to the church, we started inviting our neighbors to have ice cream on our front lawn.

The last several years, we have hosted one of these gatherings in our front yard during Labor Day and invited neighbors over to have a pancake breakfast together. This one simple invitation has allowed us into our neighbors' lives, something we did not yet have relational access to. We have recently moved, and a few weeks before Labor Day, my oldest daughter said, "Where are we going to cook pancakes?" She sees this as a way of life rather than an addition to our calendar.

As our family has grown, we have looked for what is normal in our week and attempted to invite others into our family rituals and habits. We have a family habit of cooking homemade biscuits together on Saturday morning. I distinctly recall a Saturday in December when the Spirit impressed upon me that this was more than biscuits. This particular Saturday, we had three different neighbors who happened to be outside, and a quick invitation to grab a biscuit was met with warmth and gratitude. Over time, this ritual has grown into an extended family of friends and neighbors who come and go, sharing life and biscuits.

Look through your week and open your door to neighbors and friends to share life and share food.

## Generosity

In the book *The Art of Neighboring*, Jay Pathak suggests trying to become the neighbor who is always willing to help. There is almost always someone working on their house, cleaning up the yard, or repairing a car or lawnmower. Pay attention, notice what is going on, and see if you can lend a hand. Build a reputation of making your tools available for use and become a handy-dandy-helpful-Hal resource. To get started, you might take some time to get to know the people around you. Take frequent walks, talk with people you encounter, get to know their names, and learn their stories. As you talk, you may hear opportunities to offer assistance, lend a tool, or share something you own. When you share, don't worry about getting it back and don't be concerned if it's broken or damaged. It's just stuff.

## Friendship

Adopt the mindset of building friends and growing relationships. With every interaction and conversation, your relationships will grow. Strangers will become acquaintances, acquaintances will become friends, and friends will become part of the family. Just as we can be hospitable and invite others to share our lives and join in our routines, we can also learn to join others in their routines. As you grow friends, enjoy spending time with them, be interested in what they are interested in, and take a genuine interest in their life. Go to their kids' concerts, ball games, or recitals. Include them in your celebrations and join theirs when invited. Rejoice when they rejoice and mourn when they mourn. The challenge is to be the one willing to nudge the relationship forward by hospitality, genuine interest, mutual affection, and generosity of time.

## Conclusion

Remember that these are just a few ways we can engage the praxis of listening to God through mission. Our goal in all of this is to listen to God and believe that each and every relationship is a vehicle for us to encounter God in new ways. In this way, our neighbors can also be ambassadors for God.

# 4-Hour Silence and Solitude Retreat

## Introduction:

Thomas Merton once said, "There is no greater disaster in the spiritual life than to be immersed in unreality, for life is maintained and nourished in us by our vital relation with realities outside and above us." It is my belief that within silence and solitude, unreality is exposed, and reality comes into clearer view.

We all have things that we deny, suppress, or hide, and masks that we wear. Resting with God in silence and solitude allows us to take those masks off, place our shadow in front of us, and be completely open and vulnerable to God. It is in this vulnerability and openness where we are reintroduced to the identity of our true self before God.

## Logistics:

Choose a 4-hour block of time where you can be fully present and attentive to God. It is important that it is a time when you are "at your best" and able to commit to the exercise without distraction or fatigue. Pick a place where distractions are limited and where you can completely turn your attention towards God. I would encourage you to leave your house, go outside, and reconnect with nature.

### What to Bring: (Simplicity is the key)
Bible (physical not digital)
Journal
Pen
Snacks or pre-made meal
Water bottle
Weather appropriate clothes and supplies

### What Not to Bring:
Electronics (or have them switched off)
Books besides the Bible

Do not use the time for sermon or class prep

Alcoholic products

Suggested Schedule (feel free to do what you want, but here is an example schedule to give you a starting place):

**8am – 9am-** Spend the first hour simply being quiet. Give yourself permission to sit in the awkwardness and unproductiveness of silence. Resist the need to pray a formal prayer but learn to simply sit in the presence of God.

One of the things I do during this time is to take a deep breath in and listen for God to say, "I love you" and then exhale the breath and tell God, "I love you too." I also pick a word that draws my attention to God like: "love," "beloved," "Christ," etc. and when I feel myself getting distracted, I say that word until my attention is back on God. I also imagine myself sitting at the shore and pretend that the random thoughts that come into my mind are boats that are passing by. I recognize those boats, but I do not dwell on them. I let them pass by, and I turn my attention back to God.

**9am – 10am-** Go for a walk and spend time talking to God about the masks you wear and the things you try to hide, deny, or suppress. Be honest with God about what you think and feel about your mask or shadow. Listen for God's acceptance and love.

**10am – 11am-** Spend time reading the word. Try to read for transformation and not just information. Instead of simply reading the words, allow the words to wash over you. Don't be afraid to read a passage or chapter multiple times. As Dallas Willard has said, "It is better in one year to have ten good verses transferred into the substance of our lives than to have every word of the Bible flash before our eyes." Don't just ask "What is the text saying?" Ask instead "What is the text saying to me?"

**11am – 12am-** Write in your journal prayers, reflections, and insights about your time with God. Use the pen and paper to externalize your thoughts and be totally transparent with God and yourself. End with a few more minutes of silent meditation before leaving your retreat spot.

## Conclusion:

Brennan Manning has said, "In the act of silence you're not waiting for God to make a move. You're becoming aware of the moves he is making." Silence and solitude are habits, disciplines, or practices that we enter to learn how to be ourselves again. It is only in these times of total awareness that we can be honest with ourselves about what we have become and who God has called us to be in Him.

# Yielding to God

*By Jeremy Hoover*

Our view of discipleship is shaped by the culture of religious expectations. The prevailing expectations of my youth focused on Bible knowledge, growth in areas of serving the church, and general morality. As a result, I viewed spiritual growth as being a better example, taking ownership of different parts of worship, and eventually, teaching Bible classes.

Given this culture, it's not surprising that my career thoughts led me to focus on Biblical studies and ministry. I wanted to be able to teach others about the Bible. Although I had been a Christian for many years, my studies caused me to engage the Gospels, and as I did, my expectations about discipleship began to change. They changed because I began to see that Jesus had his own expectations and culture about discipleship—and that those things focused on following him, obeying his commands, leaving our own agendas behind, and living for a greater purpose.

One moment in Jesus' life really hit me in my senior year of college. I was preparing a lesson on Jesus' time in Gethsemane when I noticed, seemingly for the first time, Jesus' prayer: "Father, if you are willing, take this cup from me; yet not my will, but yours be done" (Luke 22:42, NIV). Jesus made known his will to the Father ("take this cup from me") but completely relinquished his own will for the sake of God's will ("not my will, but yours be done").

Jesus yielded to God for the sake of something bigger than himself. Paul also mentions this in Philippians where he says that Jesus "did not consider equality with God something to be used to his own advantage; rather, he made himself nothing" (Phil 2:6–7, NIV). Paul then showed how, as a disciple of Jesus, he himself learned from Jesus' example to yield his own life, ministry, and decisions to Jesus. Later in the same letter, he wrote about considering everything as loss for the sake of knowing Jesus and learning contentment in all things as a servant of Jesus. For me, the idea of progressively yielding my life over to God's purposes meant replacing the morality-participation view of discipleship

71

from my youth with a more fluid approach of yielding decisions to God and his will.

Yielding to God can be a difficult "next step" for contemporary Christians in part because the North American church culture expects little more than attendance, political positions, and basic moral behavior. Giving God complete control of your life is rarely held out as the ideal for all Christians to follow.

I remember a conversation I had with a member of a rural church. He was concerned that the young people in the church, over several generations, would graduate from high school, go away to college, and never come back. He believed the church suffered as a result. I told him that I believed we needed to begin teaching our youth that their Christian community was more important than their career—that we should encourage our youth to attend college locally with a view towards working locally and staying a part of our church. The gentleman was confused and wondered how the kids would make a good living without leaving to go to school and build a career. When we yield to God, our lives may end up looking drastically different than we can imagine.

My family recently underwent a major change in which we yielded to God. We left a comfortable and good life working with a well-adjusted church to become missionaries in my home country of Canada. No one but me had ever lived in Canada before, and this was a big change. But as we practiced the disciplines we've looked at in this cohort—reflective reading, listening prayer, journaling—it became clear that God was calling us to this change, and so we yielded to him and followed.

Jesus' culture and expectation of discipleship is knowing him (Jesus), not about him, and in knowing him, to then yield to him. Jesus provided many examples of how we can yield to him. In Luke, we see the following ways we can yield to him: Self-denial (8:23–26); Following (9:57–62); Obedience (10:1–12); Prayer (11:1–13).

To those who wanted to bask in their self-righteousness, Jesus told the parable of the Good Samaritan; and to those who followed Jesus to be part of the crowd, he told them to count the cost of following him. Jesus continually called those who wanted to follow him to leave things behind and to take on something new. This is what discipleship is at its core—relinquishing to God, yielding to him, day-by-day, moment-by-moment, and even decision-by-decision. It is a learned process that is aided by spiritual practices that help us listen and attend to God's leading. Then, having discerned God's will, to have the confidence to step into a new way of life, trusting that the new life in Jesus (the true identity and label given to us in Christ by God) is enough to sustain us.

Consider the following areas of life and ponder the ways God is calling you to yield to him:

**Decisions about money and time**—how you spend money and time in light of God's mission and call.

**Decisions about jobs, careers, and family**—how your job, career, or family serve the mission of God.

**Decisions about ministry**—who and where you serve.

**Life purpose and calling**—how and into what God is calling you.

# Reflection Questions

## Identity-Action

1. How can I trust my "new heart" and "new Spirit" more?

2. What prevents me from claiming God's declaration of righteousness?

3. How can I create space in my day to connect more deeply with God?

4. What can I do to remind myself of who I am in Christ?

5. What would change if I relied more on the power of the Spirit to change me?

6. How do I attempt to maintain an identity in the eyes of others?

7. In what ways do I measure my worth by comparing myself to others (at home, at work, at church, within family)?

8. How would I complete the sentence, "I am significant because …"?

9. How would my treatment of others change if I believed that I am truly righteous?

10. If I fully claimed my identity in Christ what would be different?

## Self-Spirit

1. In what ways do I need to rely on the Spirit more for transformation?

2. Why do I resist submitting to the Spirit?

3. How would my life be different if I focused on submission versus obedience?

4. What behaviors are not aligned with my new identity in Christ?

5. Where do I sense that the Spirit is leading me?

6. Why do I rely upon my own ability to grow and change?

7. What would I have to change to "set my mind" on the Spirit more often?

8. In what circumstances am I not allowing the Spirit to lead?

9. Why am I hesitant to let the Spirit lead?

# Reflection Questions

## Margin-Mission

1. How much margin exists in my week?

2. What does my schedule say about my priorities?

3. What can I give up in order to have time for mission?

4. What am I putting off till I have more time?

5. In what ways has my schedule hindered my ability to listen to God?

6. What is one thing I can do to leave more room for God and others?

7. Who are the people God is leading me to?

8. What is the next step to sharing life with those in my network or neighborhood?

## Decisions-Calling

1. What decisions do I need to yield to God?

2. What areas of life do I allow God to control? What areas do I keep for myself?

3. How do I leave room for God when making a decision?

4. Where do I resist letting God control my choices?

5. What family choices do I need to yield?

6. In what ways do I sense God calling me to serve the kingdom?

7. Who are the people that God is placing on my heart?

8. Where do I need to let go and let God lead?

9. What decisions did I make on my own today without listening to God?

10. How is my lack of faith preventing me from following a path God is revealing/has revealed to me?

# Notes

[1] Mike Breen, *Continuous Breakthrough* (Pawleys Island, SC: 3DM Publishing, 2009).

[2] Ruth Haley Barton, *Pursuing God's Will Together* (Downers Grove, IL: InterVarsity Press, 2021).

[3] Keith Beasley-Topliffe, *Surrendering to God: Living The Covenant Prayer* (Brewster, MA: Paraclete Press, 2001).

[4] IBID.

[5] Christopher Jamison, *Finding Sanctuary: Monastic Steps for Everyday Life* (Collegeville, Minnesota: Liturgical Press, 2006), p. 64.

[6] Dwelling in the Word is a practice developed by Church Innovation for the purpose of missional discernment.

[7] Kenneth Boa, *Conformed to His Image: Biblical and Practical Approaches to Spiritual Formation* (Zondervan, 2001), p. 83.

[8] Houston Heflin's *Pray Like You Breathe: Exploring the Practice of Breath Prayers* (Creek Bend Press, 2017) is a great starting place. In this short handbook, he lists many sentences from the Psalms that can be used as breath prayers.

[9] Found in *Soul Feast: An Invitation to the Christian Spiritual Life* (WJK Press, 1995) by Marjorie J. Thompson. Thompson credits Ben Campbell Johnson from his book *Invitation to Pray.*

[10] Adapted from exercise found in *Holy Silence: The Gift of Quaker Spirituality* (Paraclete Press, 2005) by J. Brent Bill.

[11] J. Brent Bill, *Holy Silence: The Gift of Quaker Spirituality*, p. ix.

[12] Adapted from questions found in Richard Foster's *Prayer: Finding the Heart's True Home* (Harper San Francisco, 1992), p. 157.

Made in the USA
Monee, IL
21 August 2022